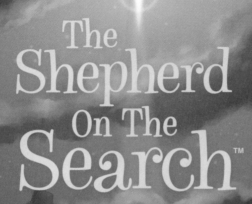

The
Shepherd
On The
Search™

By Josh Helms

25-Day Family Devotional

TO:

_____

_____

FROM:

_____

_____

_____

DATE:

_____

Shepherds were in the fields nearby watching their sheep. An angel of the Lord stood before them. The glory of the Lord was shining around them, and suddenly they became very frightened. The angel said to them, "Don't be afraid, because I am bringing you some good news. It will be a joy to all the people. Today your Savior was born in David's town. He is Christ, the Lord." — LUKE 2:8-11

TABLE OF CONTENTS

Have you ever wondered why we celebrate
the baby Jesus at Christmastime?
Or why we sing songs about a star,
some wise men, and shepherds like me?

I know I sure have!

Wouldn't it be great to discover the answers to these questions and more together?! Well, guess what...that's what this book is all about! We are going to have so much fun as we learn about what Christmas really means!

Have you ever read about the search I went on to find the baby Jesus? I hope so! I can't wait to spend some more time with you every day to talk about what I learned on my journey as well as what the Bible has to teach us about Christmas and God's amazing love. Plus, I'll be giving ideas for some fun activities that will help us learn even more! Just like Christmas, this book is for the whole family to enjoy, so I hope you'll make some great Christmas memories as you do it together!

Are you ready to get started?! Well, let's go!

A Really Big Promise

DECEMBER 1

*But the Lord Himself will give you a sign: The virgin will be pregnant. She will have a son. –*ISAIAH 7:14

I wonder how long God had been thinking about sending baby Jesus to Bethlehem. Aren't you a little curious too?! Do you think this might have been part of some great big plan that God had been working on for a long time? I know for sure that God had shared His plan with an angel before that night because the angel that visited us got so excited when he told us about it! Then all the other angels joined in making lots of noise and praising God! I think God must've told some of the old prophets, too, because a long time ago they started writing things down about how God

> ## God was making a promise—
> ## a really big promise!

was going to send a Savior. It's neat to be reading the Bible and suddenly find something about Jesus way before He ever came! God was making a promise—a really big promise—that He was going to send a Messiah, a Savior, Jesus!

Let's Search the Bible

The "Yes" to all of God's promises is in Christ....God is the One who makes you and us strong in Christ. God made us His chosen people. He put His mark on us to show that we are His. 2 CORINTHIANS 1:20-21

God told about His promise to send a Savior in many different places in the Bible. He didn't want us to miss it! Did you know that one of the people God told about His promise, Isaiah, wrote about the birth of Jesus around seven hundred years before it happened?

When God makes you a promise, you can believe it!

Seven hundred years! God's people had been waiting and praying for the coming of their Savior for a long, long time. The Bible says the "Yes" to all of God's promises is Jesus. Sometimes people promise things that never happen, but not God—when He makes you a promise, you can believe it. Jesus is proof!

Find out more: Romans 1:2-3, Romans 4:16, Titus 1:2, 1 John 2:25, Psalm 89:34, Hebrews 10:22-23.

Let's Live Out God's Word Together

During this time that leads up to Christmas, think about one promise you can keep every day. Here are some examples: "I promise to do something helpful for someone every day to show them God's love." "I promise to do my chores with a smile to show God I'm thankful that He takes such good care of me."

Find a place to put your family's promises where you all can see them every day as a reminder. Then when you see someone keeping their promise, tell them, "Good job!"

Dear Jesus, You are the proof that God kept His really big promise! Help us learn how to keep our promises too. And help us remember that God's great plan is for everyone to know that You have come! Amen.

Small Town Hero

DECEMBER 2

But you, Bethlehem Ephrathah, are one of the smallest towns in Judah. But from you will come one who will rule Israel for me. He comes from very old times, from days long ago. MICAH 5:2

Most of the time, shepherds spend their days out in the country—that's where the munchy green grass is and that's what our hungry sheep like! Can you imagine if I led my flock right through the middle of a busy town? The people wouldn't like that, and neither would my sheep—towns are for people, not sheep! Lots of things happen in towns. Did you know Jesus was born in a small town? After the great big announcement we

> Great things can come from small places.

heard from the angels, I was surprised to see how small Bethlehem really was. It's pretty special that someone as great as Jesus could come from a place so small. That just shows how amazing God is, don't you think? I guess it doesn't matter where you're from, because God can still do great things through you!

Let's Search the Bible

The Lord said to Samuel, "Go! Appoint him. He is the one." So Samuel took the container of olive oil. Then he poured oil on Jesse's youngest son to appoint him in front of his brothers. From that day on, the Lord's Spirit entered David with power. 1 SAMUEL 16:12-13

Did you know someone else famous came from Bethlehem besides Jesus? The shepherd boy that became a king, David, was from the same town! Right there in Bethlehem, Samuel appointed

> God uses little things in big ways.

David to become the King of Israel when he was just a young boy still shepherding his father's flock. Many years later the King of Kings, Jesus, was born there. Bethlehem was just a small town in those days but God used it in big ways! God cares more about where you are going than where you came from. When you put your faith in God, you can do big things!

Find Out More: 1 Samuel 16:1-13, Micah 5:2-5, John 7:42, 1 Timothy 4:12

Let's Live Out God's Word Together

The way that Jesus came tells us a lot about God. He came in a very humble way from a very humble place, yet He did great big things. Have you ever thought about your home town? How many people live there? Has anything really important ever happened there? Was anyone famous born there? Spend some time together talking about where you're from. You might learn some fun things you didn't know!

Dear Jesus, thank You for the way You came to earth—to a small town, but to do great big things. Help us learn to trust You to do big things through us too. Amen.

Give
God the
Glory

Then Mary said, "My soul praises the Lord." LUKE 1:46

I'm pretty sure that my sheep really like me. You know why? They sure get excited when I give them the sign it's time to get going out to the pasture. They kind of have a contest to see who can walk right next to me—like I'm somebody famous they want to be with! Then after they've eaten their fill of fresh green grass, some will come over and rub my leg as if to thank me for the yummy meal. Do you like it when someone makes

> We praise God when we make a
> big deal over how great He is.

a big deal over being with you or because of something special you've done for them? Do you think God likes it when we make a big deal over how great He is and all the awesome things He's done for us?

Let's Search the Bible

Then Mary said, "My soul praises the Lord; my heart is happy because God is my Savior. I am not important, but God has shown His care for me, His servant girl. From now on, all people will say that I am blessed, because the Powerful One has done great things for me. His name is holy." LUKE 1:46-49

The Bible is full of people giving praise to God for all kinds of reasons—like having a good harvest, hearing good news from His word, winning a victory. Mary showed us a great example because she gave God praise for who He is and what He's done—being her

We were made to give God praise.

Savior, caring for her, and choosing her for such an important job of being Jesus' mother. Did you know we were made to give God praise? Ephesians 1 says, "In Christ we were chosen to be God's people....so that we would bring praise to God's glory." That's why it makes our hearts extra happy when we praise the Lord!

Find Out More: 1 Chronicles 16:23-36, Psalm 150:1-6, Ephesians 1:3-6,11-12, Revelation 7:9-12

Let's Live Out God's Word Together

Just like He did for Mary, God has done great things for us and we want to remember to give Him thanks and praise in return. Do you ever sing praise songs at church? Singing to God can be a great way to tell Him how thankful we are for all He's done for us. Choose one of your family's favorite Christmas carols and look at the words for different ways of giving praise to God. Then sing the song together and give Him praise from a happy heart!

Dear Jesus, we're so thankful for all You've done for us, especially that You came for us. Please help us to always remember to give You all the praise and glory You deserve. Amen.

Say
Yes!
to God

DECEMBER 4

Mary said, "I am the servant girl of the Lord. Let this happen to me as you say!" Then the angel went away. LUKE 1:38

Can I tell you something you might not know? Sheep can be a little bit stubborn! Sometimes, I try to move them one way, and they decide they want to go a different way. But, guess what, there might be trouble waiting for them the other way that they want to go. That's why it's important that they listen to me and follow what

> It's important to learn to say, "Yes!"

I say. I love them and want what's best for them so I would never try to put them in danger. Do you have anyone in your life who looks out for you like that? They love you so much and when you say, "Yes!" to them when they ask you to do something, it's just like a picture of saying, "Yes!" to God!

Let's Search the Bible

Trust the Lord with all your heart. Don't depend on your own understanding. Remember the Lord in everything you do. And He will give you success. Don't depend on your own wisdom. PROVERBS 3:5-7

What do you think would have happened if Mary had said, "No," to God? Remember that she was young, she wasn't married, and she probably had plans of her own. Then all the sudden an angel shows up and changes her whole life—her whole world! It might have been easy to say, "No thanks, I already have my plans," but she didn't. Instead, she said, "Yes!" to God. And because she trusted God's plan more than her own, she brought into the world our Savior. Guess what—God has plans for your life too! He loves you and wants to help you grow and shine for Him. He has things for you to do—not always easy things, or maybe not the things you have in mind—but great things. He wants more for you than you could ever imagine—which is a really great reason to say, "Yes!" to Him!

Find Out More: Jeremiah 29:11, Ephesians 2:8-10, 6:1-3, 1 John 2:3-6, Deuteronomy 28:1-14, Isaiah 6:8

Let's Live Out God's Word Together

Can you think of someone God has put in your life to look out for you? Your parents! Not only should we obey them, but we should do it joyfully. The next time your parents ask you to do something, like cleaning your room or taking out the trash, answer them with a joyful "Yes!" You might just be surprised how doing something with a joyful heart can change how you feel about the whole thing!

Dear Jesus, thank You for loving us and coming to us to give our lives a new purpose. Help us to say, "Yes!" to You every day to show the world that we are Yours! Amen.

Immanuel, God With Us

DECEMBER 5

"The virgin will be pregnant. She will have a son, and they will name him Immanuel." This name means "God is with us." MATTHEW 1:23

When the angels told us shepherds about Jesus in the field that night, I knew there must be something special about Him. As I got closer and closer to where Jesus was I could actually start to feel it. Then, when I finally got to see Him, I couldn't stop looking at Him and thinking about

> God's love makes your
> heart feel brand new.

how amazing He was. Have you ever felt that way? Can you just imagine actually looking at the face of Jesus?! It was the most incredible feeling! And you know what else I thought as I looked at that special baby? Right here—this is love, perfect love, God's love. I wanted that love in my heart! I knew in that moment that God's perfect love can make your heart feel brand new. I'm so glad I was able to get so close! Believe me, when you get close to God, you won't ever want to leave!

Let's Search the Bible

Now God's home is with men. He will live with them, and they will be His people. God Himself will be with them and will be their God. REVELATION 21:3

Doesn't it make you feel special when someone you really like shows you that they want to be with you and do special things with you? Grandmas and Grandpas can be like that! Did you know that in the very beginning of the Bible God was with Adam and Eve in the garden? Not just above them or around them but

God had a plan to be with us again.

WITH them! After Adam and Eve sinned they couldn't stay in the garden with God anymore. But, God had a plan to be with us again—Jesus is His plan! Christmas is about Jesus being God with us. And because of Jesus we can be with God now and forever!

Find Out More: John 1:10-14, Romans 8:37-39, Genesis 3:24, Revelation 21:1-7, Revelation 21:22-27

Let's Live Out God's Word Together

Do you have someone in your life that loves spending time with you? Maybe a brother or sister or best friend? God places people in our lives like that because He loves us so much. Think of that person in your life and find a way to spend some quality time with them. This could be anything from coloring, doing a puzzle, making something, or spending some time talking. They'll feel special because you took time for them, and you'll feel special too!

Dear Jesus, thank You for fulfilling God's plan to be with us. Help us to always remember to love You and those around us with Your special kind of love. Amen.

What's In A Name

A child will be born to us. God will give a son to us. He will be responsible for leading the people. His name will be Wonderful Counselor, Powerful God, Father Who Lives Forever, Prince of Peace. ISAIAH 9:6

Have you ever seen a flock of sheep together? I wonder if you could tell them apart. If you're not looking closely, they might all look the same— you might miss the little differences that make them each unique. Well, guess what—I can tell all my sheep apart! I spend so much time with them that I know each one really well. And you know what else? I give each of

> Our names help make us feel special.

them a name that fits their personality. I think it makes my sheep feel special when I call them by their name. Doesn't it make you feel good when someone takes the time to learn your name? Your name is a big part of who you are and a big part of who God is too!

Let's Search the Bible

The angel said to her, "Don't be afraid, Mary, because God is pleased with you. Listen! You will become pregnant. You will give birth to a son, and you will name Him Jesus. He will be great, and people will call Him the Son of the Most High. The Lord God will give Him the throne of King David, His ancestor. LUKE 1:30-32

What is the first thing that people usually learn about you when you meet them? Your name! Did you know that God told Mary what to name her baby? The very first thing the angel Gabriel

God picked out the perfect name for His Son.

told Mary about her Son was what to name Him. Names are very important to God and He picked out the perfect name for His Son. Jesus means 'Savior' and that is exactly what Jesus is—the Savior who saves us from our sin. Everything about Jesus fulfills God's plan for us, including His name. What a perfect name!

Find Out More: Luke 1:31, Matthew 1:20-21, Acts 4:12, Philippians 2:9-11, Hebrews 13:20, Revelation 22:13, Acts 4:36, Matthew 16:17-18

Let's Live Out God's Word Together

Did you know that every name has a meaning? God named His Son Jesus because He was sent to be our Savior. In the Bible names are very important because they meant something special. Let's find out what your name means! With the help of a parent, find out what your name means and spend some time talking about why it is so perfect for you. Then talk about the names for Jesus in Isaiah 9 on the other page and why they are so perfect for Him.

Dear Jesus, help us to know You better as we learn about Your names. And help us to always remember that the power to save is in Your name. Amen.

Who Needs A Savior

DECEMBER 7

The angel said, "Joseph…don't be afraid to take Mary as your wife. The baby in her is from the Holy Spirit. She will give birth to a son. You will name the son Jesus. Give Him that name because He will save His people from their sins." MATTHEW 1:20, 21

Can you imagine hearing from the time you're really little that something big and important is going to happen, and then actually seeing it when it finally does? For Joseph, he even got to be a part of it! For me, I'd heard about God's promised Messiah all my life. The shepherds often shared what the Scriptures said about the Savior while we sat under the stars at

> People wanted a Savior to change things.

night and lots of people prayed about His coming. People sure wanted someone to change things—being under the rule of the Roman government was tough. We all thought the Savior was going to make everything instantly better. That's what Saviors do, right?

Let's Search the Bible

In the past we were foolish people, too. We did not obey, we were wrong....But then the kindness and love of God our Savior was shown. He saved us because of His mercy, not because of good deeds we did to be right with God....He saved us by making us new through the Holy Spirit...through Jesus Christ our Savior. TITUS 3:4-6

Lots of people were hoping for a Savior who would change what they didn't like about the things that other people did, especially what the Romans did. The Bible talks about those kinds of changes, but there are promises about a more important kind of change—a changed heart within us! Jesus came to save us from having hearts that don't want to do what's right—that don't want to follow God. He came to give us new hearts through the Holy Spirit. When our hearts are new because of the Savior, we can share His love and that helps change everything else!

Find Out More: 1 John 4:14, 1 Timothy 2:3-4, Psalm 51:7-10, Jeremiah 24:7, 2 Corinthians 5:17, Ezekiel 36:25-27, Romans 1:16, Romans 8:38-39, Isaiah 45:21-23, Luke 24:45-47

Let's Live Out God's Word Together

Because knowing the Savior changes our hearts, let's do an activity that shows what that looks like! With the help of an adult, cut out a big paper heart and draw a line down the middle. On one side, put words or pictures that show what our hearts are like before God changes them. On the other side, put words or pictures that show what our hearts are like after God makes them new. Galatians 5:22, 23 is a good place to start for what's in a new heart!

Dear Jesus, Thank You that You knew best what kind of Savior we needed. Help us to follow You in our hearts and to let Your love show through us at Christmas and always. Amen.

Humble
Beginnings

DECEMBER 8

While Joseph and Mary were in Bethlehem, the time came for her to have the baby. She gave birth to her first son. There were no rooms left in the inn. So she wrapped the baby with cloths and laid Him in a box where animals are fed. LUKE 2:6-7

After being out in the fields taking care of the sheep, it's sure nice to get back into the warm stable. It's especially fun to snuggle up with all the lambs! Stables can be smelly, but I'm used to it now. Have you ever smelled the animals in a barn? The rooms in houses where visitors stay don't smell like that! You know what? I actually like the smell now because it's real. It's not

> Stables can be smelly, but I like it!

fancy. Mary and Joseph sure didn't seem to mind the smell either. I guess when you're holding such a special baby it's pretty easy to forget about the uncomfortable stuff around you like animals or a smelly stable! Do you ever wonder why God chose such a humble beginning out in a stable?

Let's Search the Bible

Christ...gave up His place with God and made Himself nothing. He was born as a man and became like a servant. And when He was living as a man, He humbled Himself and was fully obedient to God. PHILIPPIANS 2:6-8

Jesus was God's Son, the Savior of the world, but His first bed was a box where animals are fed. The first people that saw Him were lowly shepherds. There was no parade with loud music and people cheering. There was no presentation with very important people

Jesus is the Savior for all kinds of people.

around. There wasn't even a room reserved for Him. There was just a baby in a barn. Jesus came in the humblest of ways. From the start He showed us what it looks like to be a Savior for all people, not just the important or famous ones. Aren't you glad to know He came for everyone!

Find Out More: Matthew 20:28, Mark 9:33-35,
Luke 22:27, 2 Corinthians 8:9

Let's Live Out God's Word Together

Have you ever visited a petting zoo or a barn that holds animals? What did you think about the smell? It's easy to forget that Jesus was born into the world in a place like that. The next time you're at the zoo or in a place where animals are kept, take a moment to smell the air and say a little prayer thanking God for coming for all people the humble way He did. Jesus is the best example of living with humility that we could ask for!

Dear Jesus, thank You for leaving the glory of Heaven to come to earth and show us that You care about all people—small and great. Help us always come to You with humble hearts. Amen.

Mighty
Messengers

DECEMBER 9

An angel of the Lord stood before them (the shepherds). The glory of the Lord was shining around them, and suddenly they became very frightened. The angel said to them, "Don't be afraid, because I am bringing you some good news." LUKE 2:9-10

Have you ever wondered what was going on in Heaven right before the birth of baby Jesus? Something really big in God's plan was about to happen so they must've been really busy! I'm pretty sure God was getting the angels ready to come tell people that His Son was going to be born. Wow! What a great job those mighty messenger angels have—telling people about God's plan! One thing's for sure—it's a little scary when

> Angels tell people about God's plan.

angels show up right in front of you with a message from God—even if the message is good news! Your eyes get really big, your mouth opens wide, and you feel like you can't move your feet—have you ever felt like that? Do you think you'd like the kind of job angels have—telling people good news? Guess what—God says we get to help share His story of good news right where we are! All these years later, the message of Jesus is still the greatest news ever!

Let's Search the Bible

*The angel said... "Zechariah, don't be afraid. Your prayer has been heard by God." * The angel said... "Don't be afraid, Mary, because God is pleased with you." * The angel said, "Joseph...don't be afraid to take Mary as your wife." Luke 1:13, 30 Matthew 1:20*

God sent angels from heaven four different times to announce details about the birth of Jesus—the angels were kept really busy! No other earthly event had so much heavenly activity! The angels

> Angels from heaven came
> four different times.

came to talk to Zechariah, Mary, Joseph, and to the shepherds in the field near Bethlehem, where Jesus was born. They got to share some incredible news about what God was up to!

Find out more: Luke 1:5-20, Luke 1:26-38, Matthew 1:20-23, Luke 2:8-14.

Let's Live Out God's Word Together

Reporters on the TV or radio give us the news when something important happens. They have interviews with people who were there and who saw things with their very own eyes. Let's pretend we're reporters doing a news story about the angel's visit to the shepherds! Make up a few questions for the shepherds about what happened that night— like who they were with, what they were doing, what they heard, what they saw, how it made them feel, and why they think it was important. You'll get to know the story really well! Have fun doing your very own Christmas news show!

Dear Jesus, thank You for loving us enough to let us share in Your story of good news. Please help us never forget how amazing it is, to know and to share, and how great it is to be loved by You. Amen.

A Reason To Celebrate

Then a very large group of angels from heaven joined the first angel. All the angels were praising God, saying: "Give glory to God in heaven, and on earth let there be peace to the people who please God." LUKE 2:13-14

Have you ever been to a party? They're really fun, aren't they?! A party is usually a time to celebrate something great that has happened. Shepherds do that after they've sheared all the sheep! The sheep look kind of silly with no woolly coats, by the way. We have a party when the big job is done! What kinds of parties have you enjoyed? Want to hear about the best party I've ever been to?! It happened in a field one night a long time

> Parties are a celebration of something great.

ago while all of us shepherds were watching our sheep. All of a sudden, right out of the sky, an angel appeared—we couldn't believe our eyes! At first I was afraid, but the angel must have known because he told us not to be scared. He said our Savior had been born in Bethlehem and that we should go find Him! What happened next was really amazing—a whole bunch of other angels appeared and they started praising God together. You should have heard it! They were having so much fun celebrating—it was my favorite party ever!

Let's Search the Bible

Did you know there's lots of celebrating in the Bible? It's true! Jesus told the story of a man who was planning a great big party—a banquet. There were lots of people on the guest list but they didn't want to come so the man had his servants ask different people

God invites us to celebrate at His party!

who wouldn't normally be invited. The party ended up being filled with all kinds of people who were really thankful they could come. Everyone else sure missed out. In the book of Revelation, God invites all those who trust in Jesus to His banquet where we'll be celebrating and singing God's praises forever!

**Find out more: 1 Corinthians 10:31, Luke 15:10,
Luke 15:11-32, Exodus 12:14, Luke 14:15-24.**

Let's Live Out God's Word Together

Can you think of something you celebrate every year on the day you were born? That's right, your birthday! Did you know that Christmas is all about celebrating Jesus' birthday? Making birthday cards is fun because you can be creative and write a special message in them. Go ahead and make a special birthday card for Jesus that you can read to everyone when you're together on His birthday!

Dear Jesus, thank You for giving us so many reasons to celebrate, including being with You forever! Help us remember that You are the greatest gift we could ever receive. Amen.

Time
With
Family

DECEMBER 11

At that time, Augustus Caesar sent an order to all people in the countries that were under Roman rule. The order said that they must list their names in a register. LUKE 2:1

Most of the time around Bethlehem it's pretty calm without any big news. Things had gotten a lot crazier around the time of the visit from the angels the night I went to see baby Jesus, though. Lots of people had come to Bethlehem from all over. They'd been ordered to return to their home towns so they could be counted by the Romans. In fact, that's why Joseph and Mary were there. One good thing for me was getting to see some of

There's nothing quite like being with family!

my faraway family that had come in. That didn't happen very much so we always made a big deal of it when it did! Do you look forward to getting to see family that you haven't seen for a while? I know I sure do! Once I find out they're coming, I start thinking about being together and all the fun we'll have! There's just nothing quite like being with family!

Let's Search the Bible

The Lord is great. He is worthy of our praise...Parents will tell their children what You have done. They will retell Your mighty acts, wonderful majesty and glory. And I will think about Your miracles. They will tell about the amazing things You do. PSALM 145:3-6

Some of the things that make family time special at Christmas are yummy treats, all the lights and decorations, and of course, the gifts. But one of the best things of all is just taking time to hear family sto-

> **Families are for sharing about the good things God has done.**

ries that bring laughter and smiles. The Bible talks about how families are one of the best places to share about the good things God has done. The Lord told His people to be careful to teach their kids and grandkids the really important things about loving God and loving others. When your family time includes your own stories about God's goodness in your lives, it's filled with a special kind of joy!

Find Out More: Deuteronomy 6:5-7, Matthew 18:20, 2 Timothy 1:3-5

Let's Live Out God's Word Together

Christmas is a great time for having fun with our families. Here's an idea: Take an evening to have the little ones act out the Christmas story! With a little preparation and a few quick costumes, like tying on a towel for a shepherd's hat, you'll have a show that's guaranteed to bring laughter and smiles! There are Scriptures that tell the Christmas story right in the back of this book.

Dear Jesus, thank You for the wonderful gift of family. Help us to have a special time together telling of Your goodness and enjoying the love we share. Amen.

Miracles, Big And Small

DECEMBER 12

The heavens tell the glory of God. And the skies announce
what His hands have made. PSALM 19:1

Have you ever thought about how big the universe is? Wow—it must be really big! Sometimes on a clear, quiet night I'll look up at the stars and wonder how big God must be to have made it all. Then I'll think about how the same mighty God that created the moon and the stars also made tiny blades of grass for my sheep to eat. I saw a lot of special things that

> Everything we see shows
> God's loving care for us.

God created while on my journey to Bethlehem. Some were big and powerful, others small and gentle. Do you think God did that on purpose—to show us how big and strong He is, but also that He is very close to us and cares about our smallest need? I sure do! Maybe that's why when He sent a Savior for our world, He came as just a tiny baby!

Let's Search the Bible

Through His (Jesus) power all things were made—things in heaven and on earth, things seen and unseen, all powers, authorities, lords, and rulers. All things were made through Christ and for Christ. Christ was there before anything was made. And all things continue because of Him. COLOSSIANS 1:16-17

Do you think Mary knew as she rocked Jesus in her arms that she was actually holding the One who created the universe? As she comforted her crying baby she was calming the same One who hung the stars and moon in the night sky and who placed planets

Mary was holding the One who made everything!

in perfect order around the sun. The hands powerful enough to hold the entire world were the same tiny hands that reached up to be held by Mary and Joseph. The One that made everything came to be a part of His creation so we could know Him better and know His love. That's a big part of the miracle of Christmas!

Find Out More: Genesis 1:1, Psalm 8:3, Jeremiah 10:12, Luke 12:6-7, Hebrews 11:3,

Let's Live Out God's Word Together

God's creation shows how much He loves and cares for us. Take a walk or a drive as a family and see how many different things you can find about God's loving care. What makes the trees special? The sun and rain? Why did God make the wind blow? Sometimes all we need to do to be reminded of God's great love for us is to open our eyes and really look!

Dear Jesus, thank You for creating such a wonderful place for us to live. Help us to always remember that even though You're big enough to create mountains and thunder, You're always close by—as close as a whisper and a prayer. Amen.

Treasure These Things

DECEMBER 13

Mary hid these things in her heart; she continued to think about them. LUKE 2:19

Sometimes, when I'm out with my sheep in a field or by a stream, I'll find little treasures. I know just where to put them, too—I hide them in my handy shepherd's pouch! I've found pretty feathers, colored stones, flowers, and even the spotted eggshell from a little bird that had hatched! Later, I like to take them out, one by one, and just look at them—they make my

> Little treasures make me think
> how much God loves me!

heart smile! They make me think about how special God made the world we live in, and how much He loves me too! Do you have things you treasure in a special way? Do they make your heart smile too?

Let's Search the Bible

The shepherds went quickly and found Mary and Joseph. And the shepherds saw the baby lying in a feeding box. Then they told what the angels had said about this child. Everyone was amazed when they heard what the shepherds said to them. Mary hid these things in her heart; she continued to think about them. LUKE 2:16-19

Imagine what Mary must have been thinking when the shepherds showed up to see her newborn son—especially after she found out that lots of angels had filled the sky and told them where to find her baby, the Savior! She knew that her baby was very special and that she was chosen by God to be His mother, but it must have been surprising to hear about it from other people too. The Bible says that when Mary heard these special things about her baby Jesus, she hid them in her heart and kept thinking about them. God loves each of us so much and if we listen and look carefully, we'll notice all sorts of special things He's done for us. We can hide these things in our hearts, and like Mary, think about God's goodness and love often!

**Find Out More: Philippians 4:8, Psalm 119:11,105,
2 Timothy 3:16-17, Psalm 73:25-26, 28 Matthew 6:20-21**

Let's Live Out God's Word Together

Can you think of something really important that we should hide in our heart? God's word! Learning and remembering verses from the Bible can help us love God better and live the way Jesus wants us to. So let's do that! Ask someone to help you find a special Scripture verse to memorize. Here are a few ideas: John 3:16, Philippians 4:13, Ephesians 4:32, Proverbs 3:5-6, Psalm 37:4, Psalm 119:105. You'll always have a special treasure with you when God's word is in your heart!

Dear Jesus, thank You so much for all the special things You do for us and for giving us Your word. Please help us to always be thankful for Your love and to love You back with our whole heart. Amen.

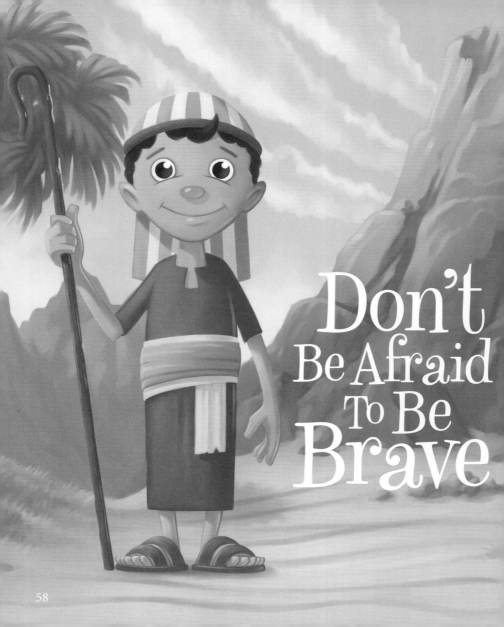

Don't
Be Afraid
To Be
Brave

DECEMBER 14

The Lord is…the one who saves me. So why should I fear anyone? The Lord protects my life. So why should I be afraid? PSALM 27:1

Shepherds are used to hearing noises while we watch over the sheep at night. We have to be ready! Sometimes robbers try to steal the sheep. I've even had to scare away lions and bears that were trying to steal a sheep from the flock! I felt a little afraid at first—okay, a lot afraid—but I soon learned that while I stay busy watching over the sheep, there is Someone who is busy watching over me. Who do you think that is? I wonder if

Never be afraid to be brave!

Joseph and Mary felt like God was watching over them as they made the long trip to Bethlehem. I'm sure they had to be plenty brave, too! Have you ever felt afraid of something—maybe something you saw, or heard, or that just popped up in your thoughts? My sheep know that I will always do everything I can to keep them safe. When I get a little scared, I tell myself, "God is with me, and when He is with me, it'll be okay!" Having courage can be kind of hard, but it's always worth it. So, never be afraid to be brave!

Let's Search the Bible

The Lord is my shepherd. I have everything I need.
He gives me new strength. I will not be afraid
because You are with me. PSALM 23:1,3-4

God knew there would be times in our lives when we'd be scared, but He doesn't want us to live in fear. Psalm 23 is about a very special shepherd, the Lord! He takes perfect care of His sheep. Did you know that's what He calls us? That's why we don't have to

God doesn't want us to live in fear.

be afraid. No matter what kind of situation you find yourself in, remember that God, your perfect shepherd, is with you, and He'll help you. If He's with you, then you have nothing to worry about!

Find out more: 2 Timothy 1:7, Psalm 23,
Psalm 27:1-5, Romans 8:31, Isaiah 41:10.

Let's Live Out God's Word Together

Have you ever watched a movie about a super-hero? They're pretty brave, aren't they?! Did you know that the biggest super heroes in our lives aren't in a movie or book? If you have a mom or dad or someone who takes care of you all the time, they are your superhero! They are always there for you, no matter what, and come to your rescue when you need them! Ask them to tell you about a time when they were scared and how they found courage. You might be surprised how brave they really are!

Dear Jesus, thank You for being our Shepherd who watches over us not just some of the time, but all the time. Help us not to be afraid but full of courage as we trust You. Amen.

Following The Star

DECEMBER 15

When the wise men saw the star, they were filled with joy. MATTHEW 2:10

I love to sleep under the stars. After the sheep have laid down for the night, I like to lie down, too, and look up at all the twinkling lights in the night sky. Have you ever done that? Aren't the stars beautiful!? What I love most about the stars is that they help to light up the darkness of the night. For us shepherds, this is a big deal! Without light, it would be too dark to protect our sheep, and protecting them is our number one job! And without the light, we

> The stars light up the darkness of the night.

couldn't see if any of our sheep have wandered off. Do you think that kind of sounds like Jesus? When He came it was just like God sending us a light so we wouldn't have to live in the dark anymore. Jesus makes everything better! I am so glad that God loved us enough to send us the light of Jesus.

Let's Search the Bible

Jesus...said, "I am the light of the world. The person who follows Me will never live in darkness. He will have the light that gives life." JOHN 8:12

Can you imagine looking up at the same sky you have seen your whole life and suddenly spotting something new—something brilliant and unexpected? This is what happened to the wise men when they saw the star of Bethlehem. They knew that this new

Jesus is the light of the world.

star must be special. God used the star to guide the wise men to Bethlehem. That bright light led them right to Jesus so they could worship Him. Jesus called Himself the light of the world. Because of Jesus we don't have to live in darkness because we have the light of life! Let's be like the wise men and always remember to let God's light guide us!

Find Out More: Matthew 2:1-12, John 1:1-5, Isaiah 60:1-5, Psalm 104:1-2, Psalm 119:105

Let's Live Out God's Word Together

Have you ever been outside on a night where you can see all the brilliant stars in the sky? Some stars twinkle a dim light and some are so bright they catch your eye right away. Here's a fun game to play with your whole family—see who can find the brightest star first! Once you've found the brightest star in the sky, say a little prayer thanking God for sending us the light of the world—Jesus.

Dear Jesus, thank You for being such a bright light in the world. Please help us to be like the wise men and follow Your light every day. Amen.

65

Turn On Your Light

DECEMBER 16

You are the light that gives light to the world. A city that is built on a hill cannot be hidden….you should be a light for other people. Live so that they will see the good things you do. Live so that they will praise your Father in heaven. MATTHEW 5:14-16

After a few nights by yourself out in the fields watching over the sheep, there's nothing better than coming over the top of a hill and seeing the lights of town to welcome you. It's not just the light you miss, of course, it's the warm beds and the time with friends and family. It's the love you feel being together. If there was no one home, the whole town would be

> Aren't you glad that light makes the darkness go away?

dark—and that wouldn't be very welcoming! One thing I've noticed—even though each house might only have one lamp shining in the window, when you put all the town's lamps together, you can see the light from far away! Do you think I'd be very bright if I was the only one who had a little lamp? What would it be like if everything was dark all the time, every day? Aren't you glad that all you need to do when it's dark is light a lamp and the darkness goes away?!

Let's Search the Bible

Be a light for other people. Live so that they will see the good things you do. Live so that they will praise your Father in heaven. MATTHEW 5:16

Have you ever tried to walk in a dark room? It's easy to bump your toe on something, isn't it? But as soon as you turn the light on, you know just where to go! As we show God's love in our lives, it's like turning the light on for people so they can see what it means

Jesus showed us how to shine with His light.

to live out God's love. The loving words we say, the kind things we do, the way we obey and help others—these are ways God's light shines from us. The good news is that we have the very best example of how to live a brightly shining life—Jesus! People are watching how we live so let's turn on our lights, then they can see Jesus' love in us!

Find out more: Matthew 5:16, 1 John 2:6, 1 Corinthians 15:33, Romans 12:2.

Let's Live Out God's Word Together

Think about how you can shine your light, right where you are. It could be something small like giving someone a special card that shows you love them or helping someone do their chores. Or it could be something big like visiting someone in a nursing home or serving food at a place where hungry people are helped. Afterwards, share with your family how it made each of you feel to shine your light so people could see Jesus' love!

Dear Jesus, please help us to be good examples to our friends and family. Thank You for being such a good example for us. Amen.

The Joy Of Giving

DECEMBER 17

The wise men…went to the house where the child was and saw Him with his mother, Mary. They bowed down and worshiped the child. They opened the gifts they brought for Him. They gave Him treasures of gold, frankincense, and myrrh. MATTHEW 2:10-11

Gifts are a very special part of Christmas. Whenever we receive a gift that someone took extra special care to find for us, it's something we treasure! Did you know that the wise men had to travel a really long way to bring their gifts when they came to see Jesus? I don't know about you, but I've never seen a real treasure up close. I imagine it would be pretty amazing though, all shiny and sparkly gold—what do you think? I kind of wish I

Giving helps make Christmas special.

could've brought something special for Jesus when I saw Him the night He was born. One thing I've learned though—there's still a way we can all keep giving to Jesus, but it isn't something we wrap with a shiny bow just for Christmas morning!

Let's Search the Bible

I was hungry, and you gave Me food. I was thirsty, and you gave Me something to drink....you invited Me into your house....you gave Me something to wear....you cared for Me.... Anything you did for any of My people here, you also did for Me. MATTHEW 25:35-36, 40

When Jesus grew up, He taught His followers a lot about giving, and one important way is by caring for others—especially those who need lots of help. In Matthew 25, Jesus told a story about a man

> We give to Jesus when we care for others.

who told some giving people that giving to others is like giving to Jesus! Christmas reminds us that God went out of His way to give His Son for us, and that shows us the best kind of giving!

Find out more: Deuteronomy 15:10, Luke 6:38, Luke 14:12-14, Matthew 25:31-40

Let's Live Out God's Word Together

Christmas is such a great time to open our hearts and give—well, any time is a great time for that! See if you can find a person or family in need and then do something special for them to help them feel God's love at Christmas. When you give to them, you'll be giving to Jesus!

Dear Jesus, thank You for being such a great example of giving to others. Help us to become more like You by being givers and helping those in need. Amen.

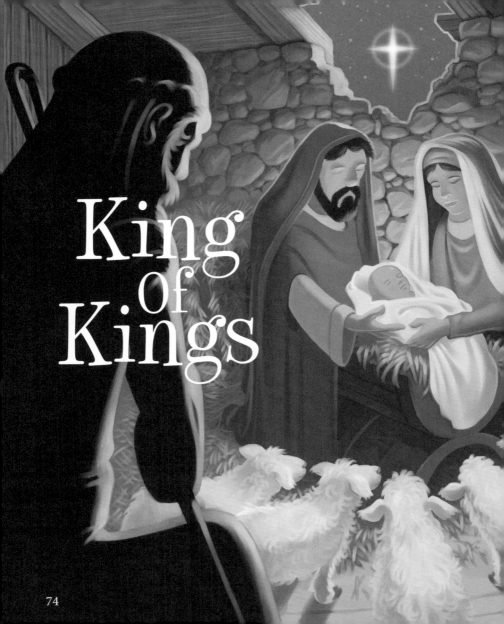

King
of
Kings

DECEMBER 18

They asked, "Where is the baby who was born to be the king of the Jews? We saw His star in the east. We came to worship Him." MATTHEW 2:22

What comes to mind when you think of a king? A royal robe and a golden crown? A fancy throne in a gigantic castle? Men blowing long trumpets while people bow down? I had some ideas about kings—but I've sure learned that not all kings are the same! A little while after seeing baby Jesus in Bethlehem, I found out that some other people had come to find Him too. The wise men hadn't heard from angels, like us shepherds, they'd

> Jesus was definitely a different kind of king!

come from afar following a special star—a star that they said was pointing them to a new and greater king. Do you think they were surprised to find that Jesus was so different than other kings—so little, and He didn't live in a castle? They hadn't come to see the crown on His head—they'd come to worship Him!

Let's Search the Bible

Power and peace will be in His kingdom. It will continue to grow.
He will rule as king on David's throne and over David's kingdom.
He will make it strong, by ruling with goodness and fair judgment.
He will rule it forever and ever. The Lord of heaven's armies will
do this because of His strong love for His people. ISAIAH 9:7

Way before Jesus came there had been king after king over the
Jewish people. They did lots of things that kings do—fighting bat-
tles with brave armies, making sure people obey the laws, meeting
kings from other countries. Some kings were good to the people,
and some weren't. Some tried to follow God, others didn't. Isaiah
the prophet told about a king to come who would always do the
right thing for his people. He would be a king everyone would
be glad to have. He would be the greatest king who would rule
forever and ever. Guess who that king turned out to be? Jesus!
When Jesus came, He told people that His kingdom was not of this
world—He would be king in a whole different way!

Find Out More: Luke 1:32-33, Matthew 2:1-12, 1 Timothy 6:15,
Revelation 19:16, Micah 5:2, Psalm 24:7-10, Zechariah 9:9,
John 12:12-15, Hebrews 1:8-9, Daniel 7:14, John 18:36-37

Let's Live Out God's Word Together

Talk together as a family: What wonderful things about Jesus, the King, are revealed in Isaiah 9:7? What can we do as a family to live like Jesus is our great King?

Dear Jesus, thank You for being a King who is always good, wise and loving. Help our lives to show that You are our King. Amen.

Holding
Onto
Hope

DECEMBER 19

Faith means being sure of the things we hope for. And faith means knowing that something is real even if we do not see it. HEBREWS 11:1

One of the scariest parts of my job as a shepherd, besides protecting my sheep from the wild animals, is helping them cross a river when we're traveling to a new meadow. I always gather them around at the edge of the river and have a little talk with them. "Okay guys, I know the water looks rough and dangerous, and you can't see the way across, but I know how to lead you through it!" Then I find the safest crossing spot and off we go. The ones who pay attention and stay close to me make it across just fine. They're all so happy! But there are always others who take off on their own way—and

> When you can't see the way, you have to hold onto hope!

that means trouble! I have to jump in and swim like crazy to get them so they don't drown! I think they hope their way is better, but it sure isn't! If they'd just stick with me, they'd be safe because their hope would be in something better than their own way!

Let's Search the Bible

Here is My servant whom I have chosen. I love Him, and
I am pleased with Him. I will put my Spirit in Him....In
Him the nations will find hope. MATTHEW 12:18,21

One of the best things Jesus brought with Him when He entered our world that night in Bethlehem was hope. Before Jesus, the world was desperate for hope—for something they couldn't see but that they could put their trust in. The good news is, Jesus not

Jesus is where we find our hope.

only brought hope, He is our hope! When we try to hold onto things other than God for our hope, it's easy to find ourselves in deep waters. But never with Jesus! The Bible also says that God gives us a hope that overflows in our lives. No matter what you're facing, never hesitate to put your hope in Jesus because He will always carry you through!

Find Out More: Isaiah 43:2, Deuteronomy 31:6,
Romans 15:13, Jeremiah 29:11, Psalm 71:5,
Hebrews 11:1-3, Romans 5:2-5, Hebrews 10:22-23.

Let's Live Out God's Word Together

Sometimes we just need to experience trusting in something we can't see to learn what hope is about. So let's do just that! Set up a little obstacle course outside, in the garage, or in a room in your house. Put down something bright red for some hot lava and make some other danger spots to be avoided. Then take turns being blindfolded and having someone direct you safely through the course. Talk about what it feels like to have to totally trust without being able to see.

Dear Jesus, thank You for the hope You bring to us every day. Help us to put our trust in You and to help others do the same. Amen.

Worth The Wait

DECEMBER 20

A man named Simeon lived in Jerusalem. He was a good man and very religious. He was waiting for the time when God would help Israel. LUKE 2:25

Have you ever had to wait for something? If you're waiting on something really good to happen it sure can be hard sometimes! Believe me there are times when us shepherds have to be very patient. Like waiting on the flock to finish at a watering hole or waiting on the sheep's wool to grow so we can have a big sheering party. I had to be patient on my journey to find

> Waiting can be hard sometimes.

baby Jesus, too. I wanted to hurry up and be there but I had to wait. Guess what? The wait was worth it when I saw Jesus! Sometimes we want things right away but I learned that it's important to wait on God's time. God's timing is always perfect and always worth it!

Let's Search the Bible

Simeon…was waiting for the time when God would help Israel. The Holy Spirit was in him. The Holy Spirit told Simeon that he would not die before he saw the Christ promised by the Lord. LUKE 2:25-26

Did you know that God's people had been waiting on a savior for a long time when Jesus was finally born? One of those people was

With God, the wait is always worth it!

Simeon, a man who always lived for God. All he wanted to do before he died was to see God's promised Savior. Having patience can be hard sometimes! But Simeon trusted God's timing and guess what—his wait was worth it! When Mary and Joseph brought baby Jesus to the temple, Simeon was finally able to hold the promised One. He told God that he could finally die in peace because he got to see the Savior with his own eyes. When we wait on God's timing, He promises to take special care of us. He loves us that much!

Find Out More: Luke 2:25-35, Psalm 37:7-9, Isaiah 40:31

Let's Live Out God's Word Together

It's hard to wait for Christmas day, isn't it? So many fun things happen on that day! Christmas is a great time to practice patience! Try this—every time you find yourself becoming anxious and wanting Christmas day to get here faster, say this: "Dear God, waiting on Your time is always worth it." This will make God smile and make waiting much easier for you.

Dear Jesus, help us to trust You like Simeon did, and to always remember that Your timing is perfect and worth the wait. Amen.

God's
Lamb

The next day John saw Jesus coming toward him. John said, "Look, the Lamb of God. He takes away the sins of the world!" JOHN 1:29

The night baby Jesus was born, the angel told us shepherds that Jesus was the Savior—Wow! I was sure curious to find out what a Savior would be like. It seemed to me that a Savior should be big and strong, like a mighty

> John said Jesus was the Lamb of God.

soldier—don't you think? But Jesus was a little baby. Of course He grew up, but He never really acted like a big tough guy. Maybe we needed a different kind of Savior after all. Jesus had a cousin named John who said Jesus was the Lamb of God. Well everyone knows lambs aren't big and strong—but there must be something really special about them if Jesus was called God's Lamb. Do you know why we needed the Lamb of God to be our Savior? Let's find out!

Let's Search the Bible

We all have wandered away like sheep. Each of us has gone his own way. But the Lord has put on Him (Jesus) the punishment for all...we have done.... But He didn't say a word. He was like a lamb being led. ISAIAH 53:6-7

Way before Jesus ever came, the Bible tells about a Savior who would not be big and strong like we might think. Before Jesus came, they used lambs to remind people they needed a savior—over and

> Jesus came to save us
> once and for all.

over again. But the good news about God's Lamb was that He came to save us once and for all. Jesus was the one and only Lamb of God. And you know what? After He died for us, He rose again with power—the kind of power that makes Him live forever—and that shows He really is a big and mighty Savior after all!

Find out more: Acts 8:26-35, Isaiah 1:18, Isaiah 53:1-12, Matthew 20:25-28, Revelation 5:6-13, 1 Peter 1:18-22, Revelation 17:14.

Let's Live Out God's Word Together

Isaiah 53 says we have wandered like sheep. Take some time to talk together about what can happen when something or someone wanders away from a safe, protected place. Then talk about what has to happen to find them and how everyone feels when they are finally found.

Dear Jesus, thank You for being the Lamb of God that takes away our sin, once and for all. Thank You for showing us Your mighty power by rising again too! Amen.

Joy To The World

DECEMBER 22

The angel said to them, "…I am bringing you some good news.
It will be a joy to all the people. Today your Savior was born
in David's town. He is Christ, the Lord." LUKE 2:8-11

I don't think I've ever felt anything like the joy that I felt when I finally saw the lights of Bethlehem come into view that night. I was so excited! For me that meant two very important things. The first was that my journey was almost over. Phew…I was ready for a rest! The bigger thing it meant

> There's a lot to be excited
> about at Christmas.

was that it was almost time to see Jesus! I had traveled a long way to see the One the angels told us about and I'd been wondering what He'd be like. Even though I was tired do you know what I did? I practically ran the rest of the way! Have you ever been that excited about something? There's a lot to be excited about at Christmas, but I don't think anything compares to the joy that Jesus brings!

Let's Search the Bible

You will teach me God's way to live. Being with You will fill me with joy. At Your right hand I will find pleasure forever. PSALM 16:11

When the angels visited the shepherds they brought good news. They said the baby born in Bethlehem would be a great joy to all the people. Then more angels appeared and they filled the sky with joyful celebration. Jesus gives us a reason to celebrate! When He is in our hearts we have joy, and that kind of joy cannot ever be

When Jesus is in our hearts we have joy!

taken away. This doesn't mean that we won't ever have times when we feel sad. Even Jesus was sad sometimes. But even when we are sad, knowing Jesus can still give us joy! Isn't it great to know that no matter what we go through or how we feel the joy that Jesus gives is stronger than anything?!

Find Out More: Galatians 5:22, Psalm 47:1, Romans 15:13, 1 Peter 1:8, Nehemiah 8:10, 1 Thessalonians 5:16-18, Luke 15:3-7, Isaiah 60:1-5

Let's Live Out God's Word Together

When people are out at the grocery store or shopping for gifts at the mall or mailing packages at the post office, sometimes they can forget about the joy that Jesus brings. Their faces don't look very happy. Let's be different and let our joy show to those around us! Saying, "Merry Christmas! The Lord has come!" with a big smile on your face is a simple way to show God's joy. The people around you might just give you a big smile back!

Dear Jesus, thank You for the joy You give that's down in our hearts every day. Please help us to always remember everything You've done for us. Amen.

Silent
Night

DECEMBER 23

Then a very large group of angels from heaven joined the first angel. All the angels were praising God, saying: "Give glory to God in heaven, and on earth let there be peace to the people who please God." LUKE 2:13-14

When I finally got into the small town of Bethlehem I was a little surprised. For a little place there sure were a lot of people! The small streets were crowded with animals and carts and people all heading different directions. It was the kind of situation that usually makes me a little nervous. Does that happen to you too? But that time I wasn't nervous at all!

> The world around us is not always a peaceful place.

In fact, I felt really peaceful—the same kind of peace I feel on a quiet night when the sheep are all safe and sound asleep. But I wasn't with my sheep and Bethlehem was not quiet that night. Why do you think my heart felt that way? The only reason I can think of is because I was getting close to Jesus. The angels talked about a peace His people would know because He came. That's because He's the only one who brings true peace!

Let's Search the Bible

I leave you peace. My peace I give you. I do not give it to you as the world does. So don't let your hearts be troubled. Don't be afraid. JOHN 14:27

Did you know that one of the names Jesus is given in the Bible is 'Prince of Peace?' There was a lot of unrest during the time that Jesus was born and God's people were ready to experience

Jesus brings true peace.

real peace. So much about the birth of Jesus speaks to that kind of peace. While outside the stable people rushed around busily, inside the stable a gentle baby lay in a manger. The shepherds came and stood in wonder as a quiet mother hid all these things in her heart. The kind of peace that Jesus brought to that busy night in Bethlehem is the same peace He wants to bring to you and me! It's the true peace that only the Prince of Peace can bring.

Find Out More: Isaiah 9:6, Isaiah 26:3, Colossians 3:15, Galatians 5:22, John 16:33, Philippians 4:6-7, Psalm 119:165

Let's Live Out God's Word Together

The apostle Paul in Colossians 3 encourages us to let the peace of Christ rule in our hearts. He wrote that while in prison—not a very peaceful place! What are some ways we can let peace rule in our hearts? Maybe by not arguing with a friend, or being kind to someone who is not kind to us? Let's talk about it! Christmas is a great time to show people the kind of peace that Jesus brings!

Dear Jesus, thank You for coming not only to bring peace but to be our Prince of Peace. Help us to always let Your peace rule in our hearts. Amen.

Prepare
Him
Room

DECEMBER 24

The shepherds said to each other, "Let us go to Bethlehem and see this thing that has happened. We will see this thing the Lord told us about." LUKE 2:15

I'll never forget how I felt the moment right before I finally arrived to see baby Jesus. The big visit from the angels, my long journey, the excitement and expectation all led right to that moment—the moment when I would finally be with the long awaited Messiah. As I stood right outside the door I took a deep breath and silently thanked God for what was about

> Take time to think about
> how good God is.

to happen. I wanted my heart to be ready. Have you ever had something happen in your life so big and important that it caused you to just stop and think about how good God is? That's all I could do in that moment—it was like I knew I would never be the same again. I guess that's what happens the first time you meet Jesus—everything changes!

Let's Search the Bible

Be still and know that I am God. I will be praised in all the nations. I will be praised throughout the earth. PSALM 46:10

When we take time to be still and really know God, He changes our lives from the inside out as we begin to trust Him to lead us, to teach us, to show us His love, and to help us do what pleases Him. As we learn more about God, we find more and more things to

> Really knowing Jesus changes us from the inside out.

praise Him for—but it takes time to get to know someone. To get to know God, you'll need to learn to have a quiet heart so you can listen for what He wants to tell you. That's how we prepare Him room in our hearts! In Hebrews 1, the Bible says God has spoken to us through His Son, Jesus, who is an exact copy of God's nature. Getting to know Jesus is definitely a great way to get to know God!

Find Out More: Hebrews 1:1-4, Colossians 2:2-3, 2 Peter 1:3, 1 Kings 19:11-12, Isaiah 40:31, Isaiah 43:18-19, Psalm 73:23-26

Let's Live Out God's Word Together

One way we could prepare room for Jesus in our hearts is to go through the chapter titles in this book, beginning with 'A Really Big Promise,' and thank God for what we've learned about Jesus so far. We don't have to do every single one, but even going through a few favorites will remind us of some pretty awesome things about God. We've been taking a journey to see Jesus and this is the last stop before we finally arrive on Christmas Day. Let's quiet our hearts and enjoy Him together.

> Dear Jesus, help us to always remember how important it is to spend quiet time with You. Thank You for loving to spend time with us. Amen.

Greatest
Gift Ever
Given

DECEMBER 25

For God loved the world so much that He gave His only Son. God gave His Son so that whoever believes in Him may not be lost, but have eternal life. JOHN 3:16

One of my favorite memories of a gift was when I received my very first shepherd's staff. I'd been hoping for one of my own for a long time because I'd seen the older shepherds with their staffs. I wasn't very tall, so my first staff wasn't very tall, either! It was kind of hard to carry for a little guy like

> God knew just the gift that the world was hoping for.

me, but I couldn't wait to use it. I just knew I'd be able to guide and protect my sheep so much better! Have you ever received a gift that you'd been hoping to receive for a long time? Or, have you ever given a gift that you knew would make someone else really happy? God knew just the right gift to give to a world that was hoping for a Savior—Jesus!

Let's Search the Bible

"The Spirit of the Lord is in Me. This is because God chose Me to tell the Good News to the poor. God sent Me to tell the prisoners of sin that they are free, and to tell the blind that they can see again. God sent Me to free those who have been treated unfairly, and to announce the time when the Lord will show kindness to His people." ...Jesus said, "While you heard these words just now, they were coming true!" LUKE 4:18-21

What the Bible says about Jesus shows that He is the perfect gift for us. When we are feeling weak He is mighty. When we feel alone He is Immanuel which means 'God with us.' When we feel hopeless He is our hope and when we feel lost He is the way. It doesn't matter what the question is, Jesus is the answer. He is proof that God loves and cares for us deeply. He doesn't want to be a faraway unreachable God, He wants to be involved in our lives. That's why He sent His Son to become one of us. Christmas is the beginning of God's never-ending love story for us!

Find Out More: James 1:17, Zephaniah 3:17, Isaiah 7:14, Psalm 71:5, John 14:6, Romans 8:38, 1 John 4:10-11

Let's Live Out God's Word Together

The chorus from "O Come, All Ye Faithful" is perfect to sing as we finally come to the manger, knowing that Jesus first came for us. "O come let us adore Him, O come let us adore Him, O come let us adore Him, Christ the Lord." *(See next page for more words.)*

Dear Jesus, thank You for Christmas. Help us to hold what it means about You in our hearts and never forget that God gave us the greatest gift we could ever receive when He gave us You. Amen.

O Come, All Ye Faithful

by John Wade

O come, all ye faithful, joyful and triumphant,
O come ye, O come ye, to Bethlehem.
Come and behold Him, born the King of angels.

Refrain

O come, let us adore Him,
O come, let us adore Him,
O come, let us adore Him,
Christ the Lord.

Sing, choirs of angels, sing in exultation;
O sing, all ye citizens of heaven above!
Glory to God, all glory in the highest.

Refrain

Yea, Lord, we greet Thee, born this happy morning;
Jesus, to Thee be glory given;
Word of the Father, now in flesh appearing.

Refrain

God Wants Us To Know The Good News That Gives Us New Hearts

Did you know that God made the world, the stars, and everything we see? When He had finished, He said it was good. He made the first man, Adam, and gave him a place to live and things to do. Adam was with God and it was very good. But something happened to the world when the man chose to disobey God. It was no longer all good, because man had sinned against God, and could no longer be with God.

Any time there is meanness, lying, hitting, disobedience, and all other sorts of bad things in the world, it's because people sin against God. Because of sin, we cannot know God in our hearts and cannot be with Him. We need a way to have new hearts so we can be with God again.

We can try to be good to get back to God, but that won't work, because there is still sin in our hearts. There's nothing we can do on our own to take away that sin. We need a Savior to help us.

The Bible says that God loves us and sent Jesus to be God with us— the Savior we need. Jesus has the power to bring us back to God. This is the good news that gives us new hearts.

How can we know from God's Word that Jesus is our Savior?

First, we understand that we have sinned.

> *All people have sinned and are not good enough for God's glory.* ROM. 3:23

Our sin leads us away from God—to death.

> *When someone sins, he earns what sin pays—death.* ROM. 6:23

But God has a way to bring us back to Him,
by giving Jesus to die for our sins.

> *Jesus was given to die for our sins.* ROM. 4:25

After He died for us, Jesus was raised from
death to make us right with God.

He was raised from death to make us right with God. ROM. 4:25

Because of what Jesus has done, we can have
the free gift of life forever with God.

God gives us a free gift—life forever in
Christ Jesus our Lord. ROM. 6:23

The choice is ours to say, "Jesus is Lord," and believe
in our hearts that God raised Him from death. When
we do that, God's Word says we are saved.

If you use your mouth to say, "Jesus is Lord," and if you
believe in your heart that God raised Jesus from death,
then you will be saved. We believe with our hearts, and
so we are made right with God. And we use our mouths to
say that we believe, and so we are saved. ROM. 10:9–11

When we have believed God's good news and trusted Jesus as our Savior, we have a new heart that begins to grow as we learn from God's Word how He wants us to live. We grow when we talk to God in our prayers, being thankful for His love, and giving Him praise. We grow when we do kind things for others to show them God's love. The most important way we show His love to people is by sharing the good news about the Savior.

God's Word says when Jesus is our Savior, nothing can separate us from God's love—ever!

Jesus is the way, the truth, and the life. He's our hope, our joy, our peace, and our perfect Friend. He's God's promise fulfilled and His greatest gift to us!

Christmas Story Scriptures

THE VIRGIN MARY

God sent the angel Gabriel to a virgin who lived in Nazareth, a town in Galilee. She was engaged to marry a man named Joseph from the family of David. Her name was Mary. The angel came to her and said, "Greetings! The Lord has blessed you and is with you."

But Mary was very confused by what the angel said. Mary wondered, "What does this mean?"

The angel said to her, "Don't be afraid, Mary, because God is pleased with you. Listen! You will become pregnant. You will give birth to a son, and you will name Him Jesus. He will be great, and people will call Him the Son of the Most High. The Lord God will give Him the throne of King David, His ancestor. He will rule over the people of Jacob forever. His kingdom will never end."

Mary said to the angel, "How will this happen? I am a virgin!"

The angel said to Mary, "The Holy Spirit will come upon you, and the power of the Most High will cover you. The baby will be holy. He will be called the Son of God. Now listen! Elizabeth, your relative, is very old. But she is also pregnant with a son. Everyone thought she could not have a baby, but she has been pregnant for six months. God can do everything!"

Mary said, "I am the servant girl of the Lord. Let this happen to me as you say!" Then the angel went away.

MARY'S VISIT

Mary got up and went quickly to a town in the mountains of Judea. She went to Zechariah's house and greeted Elizabeth. When Elizabeth heard Mary's greeting, the unborn baby inside Elizabeth jumped. Then Elizabeth was filled with the Holy Spirit. She cried out in a loud voice, "God has blessed you more than any other woman. And God has blessed the baby which you will give birth to. You are the mother of my Lord, and you have come to me! Why has something so good happened to me? When I heard your voice, the baby inside me jumped with joy. You are blessed because you believed what the Lord said to you would really happen."

MARY PRAISES GOD

Then Mary said, "My soul praises the Lord; my heart is happy because God is my Savior. I am not important, but God has shown His care for me, His servant girl. From now on, all people will say that I am blessed, because the Powerful One has done great things for me. His name is holy. God will always give mercy to those who worship Him. God's arm is strong. He scatters the people who are proud and think great things about themselves. God brings down rulers from their thrones, and He raises up the humble. God fills the hungry with good things, but He sends the rich away with nothing. God has helped His people Israel who serve Him. He gave them His mercy. God has done what He promised to our ancestors, to Abraham and to his children forever."

Mary stayed with Elizabeth for about three months and then returned home.

LUKE 1:26-56

THE BIRTH OF JESUS

At that time, Augustus Caesar sent an order to all people in the countries that were under Roman rule. The order said that they must list their names in a register. This was the first registration taken while Quirinius was governor of Syria. And everyone went to their own towns to be registered.

So Joseph left Nazareth, a town in Galilee. He went to the town of Bethlehem in Judea. This town was known as the town of David. Joseph went there because he was from the family of

David. Joseph registered with Mary because she was engaged to marry him. (Mary was now pregnant.) While Joseph and Mary were in Bethlehem, the time came for her to have the baby. She gave birth to her first son. There were no rooms left in the inn. So she wrapped the baby with cloths and laid him in a box where animals are fed.

SOME SHEPHERDS HEAR ABOUT JESUS

That night, some shepherds were in the fields nearby watching their sheep. An angel of the Lord stood before them. The glory of the Lord was shining around them, and suddenly they became very frightened. The angel said to them, "Don't be afraid, because I am bringing you some good news. It will be a joy to all the people. Today your Savior was born in David's town. He is Christ, the Lord. This is how you will know Him: You will find a baby wrapped in cloths and lying in a feeding box."

Then a very large group of angels from heaven joined the first angel. All the angels were praising God, saying: "Give glory to God in heaven, and on earth let there be peace to the people who please God."

Then the angels left the shepherds and went back to heaven. The shepherds said to each other, "Let us go to Bethlehem and see this thing that has happened. We will see this thing the Lord told us about."

So the shepherds went quickly and found Mary and Joseph. And the shepherds saw the baby lying in a feeding box. Then they told what the angels had said about this child. Everyone was amazed when they heard what the shepherds said to them. Mary hid these things in her heart; she continued to think about them. Then the shepherds went back to their sheep, praising God and thanking Him for everything that they had seen and heard. It was just as the angel had told them.

When the baby was eight days old, He was circumcised, and He was named Jesus. This name had been given by the angel before the baby began to grow inside Mary.

LUKE 2:1-21

WISE MEN COME TO VISIT JESUS

Jesus was born in the town of Bethlehem in Judea during the time when Herod was king. After Jesus was born, some wise men from the east came to Jerusalem. They asked, "Where is the baby who was born to be the king of the Jews? We saw His star in the east. We came to worship Him."

When King Herod heard about this new king of the Jews, he was troubled. And all the people in Jerusalem were worried too. Herod called a meeting of all the leading priests and teachers of the law. He asked them where the Christ would be born. They answered, "In the town of Bethlehem in Judea. The prophet wrote about this in the Scriptures: 'But you, Bethlehem, in the land of Judah, you are important among the rulers of Judah. A ruler will come from you. He will be like a shepherd for my people, the Israelites.'"

Then Herod had a secret meeting with the wise men from the east. He learned from them the exact time they first saw the star. Then Herod sent the wise men to Bethlehem. He said to them, "Go and look carefully to find the child. When you find Him, come tell me. Then I can go worship Him too."

The wise men heard the king and then left. They saw the same star they had seen in the east. It went before them until it stopped above the place where the child was. When the wise men saw the star, they were filled with joy. They went to the house where the child was and saw Him with His mother, Mary. They bowed down and worshiped the child. They opened the gifts they brought for Him. They gave Him treasures of gold, frankincense, and myrrh. But God warned the wise men in a dream not to go back to Herod. So they went home to their own country by a different way.

JESUS' PARENTS TAKE HIM TO EGYPT

After they left, an angel of the Lord came to Joseph in a dream. The angel said, "Get up! Take the child and His mother and escape to Egypt. Herod will start looking for the child to kill Him. Stay in Egypt until I tell you to return."

So Joseph got up and left for Egypt during the night with the child and His mother. Joseph stayed in Egypt until Herod died. This was to make clear the full meaning of what the Lord had said through the prophet. The Lord said, "I called My Son out of Egypt."

MATTHEW 2:1-15

JESUS IS PRESENTED IN THE TEMPLE

The time came for Mary and Joseph to do what the law of Moses taught about being made pure. They took Jesus to Jerusalem to present Him to the Lord. It is written in the law of the Lord: "Give every firstborn male to the Lord." Mary and Joseph also went to offer a sacrifice, as the law of the Lord says: "You must sacrifice two doves or two young pigeons."

SIMEON SEES JESUS

A man named Simeon lived in Jerusalem. He was a good man and very religious. He was waiting for the time when God would help Israel. The Holy Spirit was in him. The Holy Spirit told Simeon that he would not die before he saw the Christ promised by the Lord. The Spirit led Simeon to the Temple. Mary and Joseph brought the baby Jesus to the Temple to do what the law said they must do. Then Simeon took the baby in his arms and thanked God: "Now, Lord, You can let me, Your servant, die in peace as You said. I have seen Your Salvation with my own eyes. You prepared Him before all people. He is a light for the non-Jewish people to see. He will bring honor to Your people, the Israelites."

Jesus' father and mother were amazed at what Simeon had said about Him. Then Simeon blessed them and said to Mary, "Many in Israel will fall and many will rise because of this child. He will be a sign from God that many people will not accept. The things they think in secret will be made known. And the things that will happen will make your heart sad, too."

ANNA SEES JESUS

Anna, a prophetess, was there at the Temple. She was from the family of Phanuel in the tribe of Asher. Anna was very old. She had once been married for seven years. Then her husband died and she lived alone. She was now 84 years old. Anna never left the Temple. She worshiped God by going without food and praying day and night. She was standing there at that time, thanking God. She talked about Jesus to all who were waiting for God to free Jerusalem.

JOSEPH AND MARY RETURN HOME

Joseph and Mary finished doing everything that the law of the Lord commanded. Then they went home to Nazareth, their own town in Galilee. The little child began to grow up. He became stronger and wiser, and God's blessings were with Him.

LUKE 2:22-40

Here is a special place for recording any memories or significant thoughts from your family's devotional journey at Christmas.

_____

_____

_____

_____

_____

_____

_____

_____

_____

_____

_____

_____

_____

_____

_____

For Jacob and Everley —J. & L.

Special thanks to Randy Helms for his biblical wisdom and counsel.

ABOUT THE AUTHORS

From the beginning, Christmas has been a fun and exciting time at the Helms' home in Nashville, Tennessee. Josh and Lindsey, the creators of *The Shepherd on the Search*, have looked for ways to give their two children, Jacob and Everley, a sense of the wonder of the season. Like many Christian families, they've found it a challenge to keep Christ and the story of that first Christmas at the center. Out of that desire came *The Shepherd on the Search*, a fun way to keep the family conversation focused on a young shepherd who spends the weeks before Christmas looking for God's greatest gift, Jesus. Josh & Lindsey hope that He is the gift found by every heart!

ABOUT THE ILLUSTRATOR

Trent Design, Inc. is a full-service design studio specializing in branding and marketing design, as well as product development, packaging, and illustration. They are known for creating engaging and memorable visual solutions for clients such as the Walt Disney Company®, Big Idea/Dreamworks®, Herschend Family Entertainment®, DaySpring, Thomas Nelson®, Scholastic®, Dave Ramsey, Provident Films® and many others.

Jonathan Bishop is a graphic designer and illustrator, working primarily in the entertainment industry. His past experience includes many years as an artist with the Walt Disney Company®.